ENGAGE, COLLABORATE, LEAD!

Ignite Your Business and Your Life

. . .

Denise W. Barreto

Engage, Collaborate, Lead! Ignite Your Business and Your Life
Copyright © 2014 by Denise W. Barreto, a Relationships Matter Now publication

All rights reserved.
No part of this book may be reproduced or transmitted in any form or
by any means without written permission from the author.

ISBN: 1502945665
ISBN-13: 9781502945662
Library of Congress Control Number: 2014921769
CreateSpace Independent Publishing Platform,
North Charleston, South Carolina

Printed in the United States of America

DEDICATION

To Betty Jean Jackson, my dearest mom, who passed away at the tender age of twenty-four in 1976 but continues to be my inspiration to live well and enjoy life to the fullest.

CONTENTS

Foreword 1

Introduction 3

Chapter One: Engage 7

Chapter Two: Collaborate 23

Chapter Three: Lead 47

Conclusion 69

Resources 73

Acknowledgments 75

About the Author 77

FOREWORD

Think back in your life to the moment when you met someone who had an instrumental role in changing the trajectory of your life in some way. Did you realize it at the time, or have you only now realized the impact of that connection in hindsight? Often the most tenuous, delicate, and incidental overlaps end up creating the fabric from which the tapestry of our lives is fashioned.

In life, you never know when you will make just such a pivotal connection. Maybe it's a blind date that turns into a lifelong love. Or perhaps it is a chance meeting that results in a powerful mentor and cheerleader. Whatever the case, each of us impacts those around us in ways that we often fail to recognize at the time, but which prove to be profound and life changing.

I met Denise Barreto through a blogger friend in 2013. "You should connect with Denise," she said. Denise and I soon became acquaintances, colleagues, and friends.

We brainstormed, bouncing ideas off one another. We shared the ups and downs of business and professional life. We collaborated and connected.

At the end of 2013, Denise asked me to take a look at her media kit and give some suggestions as she was planning her strategy to take her business to the next level in 2014. I read through the kit, and three concepts immediately jumped out at me.

Engagement
Collaboration
Leadership

These qualities capture the magic of how Denise works and in large part demonstrate the fundamental shifts and powerful results she creates for her clients.

Engage, Collaborate, Lead defined the blueprint of Denise's own success as well as the success she helps her clients achieve. As we discussed these ideas in further detail, it wasn't long before Denise realized that she needed to capture the essentials of this simple formula to be able to share it more easily with the world. You hold the results of that effort in your hand.

Engage, Collaborate, Lead! Ignite Your Business and Your Life offers practical insights and a clear, one-two-three–step path to business success in any venue. In this blueprint, Denise shares practical advice and powerful anecdotes from her life and work that will help you engage your team and achieve success in your own business and organization.

The power of Engage, Collaborate, Lead lies in the fact that this process is not just how Denise administers her own business but is also how she lives her life. It's part of her DNA. There is no one who I know of personally who is better equipped to take you from where you are to where you want to be than Denise Barreto.

I've seen her work her magic firsthand and have experienced the Engage, Collaborate, Lead difference in my own life and business. I encourage you to delve right in and find out what a difference Engage, Collaborate, Lead can make in your life and business.

Steve Rice, Founder
SRCommunications
November 2014

INTRODUCTION

In 2008, when I set out on a journey to use my best talents every day, I had no idea where it would lead me. Frustrated and weary of my life, both personally and professionally, I took a step back to recognize what mattered most to me - and discovered it was my relationships. Casual or intimate, personal and professional - all my relationships mattered and were the fuel that made me "go." At first, I focused on repairing a relationship on the brink. Then I turned my attention to my relationship with work. I decided that right where I was, as a middle manager at a Fortune 500 corporation, I was going to use my best talents daily. What started as a simple declaration ended in the birth of a consulting business, Relationships Matter Now, founded in 2010.

Started as a side business with small projects while I continued to work full-time as a marketer at a large national retailer, Relationships Matter Now quickly picked up steam. Two small projects multiplied to many, and by the start of 2012, I'd left my middle-management post to guide my own destiny. In the early days of my company, if you had asked me what set my services apart from the competition, I'd have struggled to tell you. Now, when I look back on those first few years, it was just "hacking" out business. My heart for relationships was big, and my core belief guided me.

No good is ever accomplished without healthy, vibrant relationships between humans.

Armed with that phrase, a ton of faith, and a supportive tribe, I started building projects across many disciplines. Culture building and organizational development were the first areas in which the company made its mark. Relationships Matter Now started in this area from a love of service and parks and recreation professionals. Guest teaching at the annual Illinois Parks and Recreation Association and Illinois Association of Park Districts conference as a way to use my talents of facilitating great discussions, I quickly became a resource to help park agencies across the state that wanted to improve their work environments. Strategic planning was not far behind. As a local elected official, I saw a need for more strategic thinking around small municipal government agencies. First, I volunteered to speak at the annual Illinois Municipal League conference for elected municipal officials in the state, and I then served as a strategic planning facilitator for my peers in municipalities of less than fifty thousand residents. Board training and leadership development for elected and appointed board officials were next to surface as a need Relationships Matter Now could fill.

Marketing and branding have always had a place in the portfolio of Relationships Matter Now work as my twenty-plus-year career was grounded in the ever-changing discipline. Alongside the culture building and strategic projects, Relationships Matter Now has always had at least one to two marketing projects at a time: one for corporate entities and always one for a nonprofit agency. Finally, with all my corporate ties, inclusion and diversity strategy became the last area of work for Relationships Matter Now to enter. Citing my facilitation skills, one by one, former coworkers of mine tapped Relationships Matter Now to come and lead discussion around inclusion and diversity strategy in their new companies. Now inclusion and diversity are the fastest-growing segments of Relationships Matter Now's body of work.

Playing in so many different fields of service, figuring out how to best describe the work Relationships Matter Now does was getting increasingly difficult. And while I'm a marketer and storyteller at heart, I was struggling to clearly articulate the value Relationships Matter Now was delivering to its clients. Then, in a stroke of serendipity, I enlisted a good friend and amazing content marketer to help me update all the marketing materials for Relationships Matter Now. Throughout the creative process, we spent many hours discussing Relationships Matter Now projects—the work and methodology that were growing our client and project base.

During these exchanges, my copywriting friend studiously took notes, asked questions, and probed and prodded me to exhaustion about each of the different types of projects across the various types of organizations Relationships Matter Now served. When this exercise was finished, he promised to come back with updated, refreshed language to better tell the story of Relationships Matter Now. I had no high hopes for what this language would produce. I was only relieved that I had finally mustered up the courage to outsource something that I'd normally done for myself.

Within a week, the new language came back, and it was revolutionary for Relationships Matter Now.

Engage
Collaborate
Lead

These are three little words, yet they create a hugely powerful and differentiating phrase that succinctly and accurately describes the way Relationships Matter Now works with its clients. These words represent the brand promise Relationships Matter Now delivers every day, with every client on every project. Not only have we grown the business steadily since implementing our new brand position, I discovered that Engage, Collaborate, Lead is a living, breathing way of life for me.

This came to life for me for the first time after almost a year of using the new language at a conference at the University of Notre Dame's Mendoza College of Business. An MBA student was assigned to escort me around the conference and get me to my program contribution later in the afternoon. We spent several hours together with little time to truly talk about my company or what we did on a daily basis. In between sessions and over lunch, I had the chance to get to know this student as well as many others attending the conference that day. When it was time for my duty to facilitate a rock star panel of women executives from companies such as NBC News, GE, and Bank of America, I was blown away by the short yet succinct introduction my MBA student escort delivered to the conference.

He read three quick sentences about me and my business in typical conference biography introduction style, and then he deviated. He looked up and stated that he could easily finish reading the bio before him but decided to tell a quick story about why they were all going to be "delighted" by my work. "It's simple," he started.

"This woman lives her brand - engage, collaborate, lead. She engaged with me and many students today, and we collaborated on the topics we are tackling today, and I know I will be a better leader having spent time with her. Ladies and gentlemen, Denise W. Barreto…"

Not one moment before that did I realize how truly powerful this basic phrase was to impact people positively. It was then I decided that what comes natural to me and is a trusted methodology for my business is fully replicable for the masses. Together, we will look at how Engage, Collaborate, Lead has the power to transform any organization and enable you to take it from where it is today to where it desires to be.

Further, I believe that Engage, Collaborate, Lead has personal implications as well. As much as I live and breathe this brand promise in my business, I have also seen evidence of its success in my personal life. As we unpack this dynamic practice for our business over the coming pages, as a bonus, I've included snapshots of how Engage, Collaborate, Lead looks in personal life circumstances as well. We use it in our family quite often, and it has enhanced one aspect of our lives together greatly. You will see how this simple yet powerful process can positively impact any interactions you have with other humans you are intending to influence. Regardless of where or who you lead, we are certain that implementing Engage, Collaborate, Lead can make an immediate difference in all you do. Join me on a quick and interactive journey to transform the way you do business and the way you do life.

1

ENGAGE

One of the hottest buzzwords of the twenty-first century is the word *engage*: 2,138 nonfiction books with the word *engage* in the title have been written since the century began, and 1,737 have been written since 2007, when the social media networks were at their highest adoption and expansion phase, with over 25 percent of them targeting business, training, or organizational development.

Regardless of the industry or genre, people have tuned in to this word in a big way lately. And it's no wonder why. Look at a few definitions from the *Merriam-Webster Dictionary* for the transitive verb, to *engage*:

> *a : to entangle or entrap in or as if in a snare*
> *b : to attract and hold by influence or power*
> *c : to interlock with*
> *d : to bind (as oneself) to do something*
> *e : to hold the attention of*
> *f : to induce to participate*

These particular definitions jumped out to me as I looked at how Relationships Matter Now used the word in our work and daily interactions with our clients. The ability to attract and hold by influence is real when trying to motivate adults to action. Additionally, holding attention and inducing to participate are key elements to moving people in a direction. But the definition that comes to life for me and serves as the basis for use of the word in our brand promise is "to bind (as oneself) to do something."

Think about that for a minute. "To bind (as oneself) to do something."

When you want to motivate and drive understanding in adults, it is critical that you get them to bind themselves to your idea or concept. Over the last four years, I have intently studied adult learning models, and all of them have one thing in common: the story-to-story connection. Relationships Matter Now derives its definition of engage in just that manner. We aim to tie personal stories to the greater story an organization is building. And we believe that is the key to truly moving and driving actions in adults today.

Why Engage?

We engage because that's the way we learn. You've all heard that people love to talk about themselves. While this is true in most cases, it takes on another level when we can talk about ourselves in relation to something bigger. Back in 2010, while working for one of the largest retailers in the United States, I saw this phenomenon firsthand again and again.

As part of the toys business unit marketing team, I was challenged to lead our business unit's adoption of a "Take Your Kids to Work Day" event. With a campus of close to four thousand employees at headquarters, the idea that we could use a routine event to impact our business was not farfetched. However, it had not been done before. My thought immediately was twofold: one, timing wise, we could use this opportunity to get a glimpse of what excited kids for the upcoming holiday season before buy commitments had to be made; two, I saw this as an opportunity to drive manufacturing, marketing, and sales goals. However, getting buyers, marketers, and vendors to partner quickly was no easy task.

My first step was to convince our leadership why investing time would have a great return. Instead of creating a PowerPoint like most folks in my position, I called a meeting to ideate ideas. I remember vividly people filing in the room with the dreaded looks of "Oh no, not another brainstorm," written all over their faces. After everyone was in the room, I started with a targeted icebreaking game to transition all our attention on the task at hand - making the most out of our business unit's turn at hosting a "Take Your Kids to Work Day" event.

Then I pulled out a few toys and board games that we'd secured from a few vendors quickly. For the next twenty minutes, as a group we connected our own desire to play to the desire today's kids - our targets - have to play. The forty-five minutes after that were the most productive I've seen from a cross-functional group of people in our business unit - ever. Not only did we lay out the ninety-minute program for our kids' workshop that year, but we also figured out how to use that time for planning the following year's buys. Inventory managers, marketing specialists, and buyers left that room that day motivated to deliver a fantastic experience to our workshop participants and laid out how we could leverage this activity annually with our vendor partners.

That holiday, not only did our Toys Business Unit team hit its goals, but it also exceeded them by almost 20 percent and paid out large bonuses to our team as the rest of the company suffered through flat sales and slight increases in disparate pockets throughout the company.

The ability to mobilize the team around one idea created an environment of engagement that was rarely seen before or since that time. From that special event through the tough holiday buying and selling season, the team was bonded together around their goals. Several additional work sessions were conducted over the next eighteen months, specifically working around each buying team to drive greater connection to their goals.

To see concrete and consistent growth and change in your organization, you have to help the team connect its own story to the greater story your organization is building. Creating space to connect those stories is critical.

Most often people have very few opportunities to connect their story to a greater story. Building a culture that values stories is key. Take a few moments to look over all the current touch points that leaders in your organization have with associates. Ask yourself the following series of questions:

- How often are associates asked their opinion about our work?
- When in our processes do we gather input from affected associates?
- Do our teammates have a true bond or connection to what we are trying to accomplish?
- Can our associates articulate *our* story?

These questions are posed to get your mind around ways to engage your team to move in the direction you need to them go.

The Story

Is it amply clear to everyone in your organization why you exist? This critical question makes or breaks the ability to engage people. People must know "the story." For some organizations, this is a simple task of reinforcing a solid brand story and position again and again. For others, it means you have to simplify the story.

In the early days of Relationships Matter Now, when asked what we did, it was painful to me each and every time I had to answer that question. We do lots of things. We conduct strategic planning sessions. We deliver service-excellence training and culture-building workshops. We create strategies and strategic programming for inclusion and diversity practitioners. We develop brand and marketing strategies and tactics. Getting all those things into an "elevator speech" was daunting. We were the Proctor & Gamble of small-business consulting. It was painful, but like most entrepreneurs, we pressed forward without the story. Growth was painful but steady, and as we approached year three, it was clear we needed assistance creating our story.

As a marketer, this was a sobering yet freeing realization. Companies were hiring my company to help them tell their story, and I could not even tell our own. This is true of so many organizations. People get caught up in delivering products and services and forget the "why." Preparing to bring the content marketer up to speed on Relationships Matter Now's history to date did not open my eyes to the obvious - my utter lack of connection points for clients.

In the same way that we need to create connection points for associates within an organization, we must create connection points for the people we intend to serve. Handing over client case studies, conducting interviews, and describing our work again and again for the content specialist crystalized our story.

Relationships Matter Now is a transformative partner. Regardless of the project or industry, we use a repeatable process to drive change and results in the organizations we serve. Armed with our story, we engaged current and potential clients in connecting their story to our greater story. We saw an immediate impact once we implemented our new brand position and promise that fall. Not only did we spread our story to current and potential partners quickly, but we also made sure that key people in our personal networks knew and could articulate the story. Every team member at Relationships Matter Now owned the story and made sure it was known to his or her top connections. We are a small team of four people. Can you imagine that impact on larger organizations? In the retailer story I referenced before, true associate engagement spread across a business unit of more than sixty team members and mobilized them past their sales and profit goals that year. Understanding *the story*, *why* our team was selling toys, and connecting it to the stories of kids at our "Take Your Kids to Work Day" event and beyond solidified unity of purpose and drove excellent execution.

Take a few moments to review the first step of engaging your team - the story.

- What is your story?
- Is it clear to all members of your team?
- Can they articulate it to someone else?
- Do they understand how they can positively impact that story?

Barriers to True Engagement

Once the organization's story is solid and people understand it, there are still barriers that can prohibit true engagement that must be recognized.

Lack of sincerity from leadership is one key barrier to true engagement. People want and need to understand where they stand. Honest feedback and candor are critical to gaining the trust necessary for people to share their stories. One of Relationships Matter Now's first clients, a local government agency, had this problem. Leaders would say they wanted to hear from their associates but literally left the room right after the declaration. Not only did this create an uncomfortable situation for me as the facilitator of the discussion, it was difficult for the team to believe that anything we did would matter.

People engage when they can clearly see how their engagement will benefit them. Leaders have to walk the line of encouraging engagement while simultaneously being open to engage themselves. Often, leaders tell us that they fear truly engaging because of what they perceive their team will think of them. That resistance to appear vulnerable drives the perception of "us versus them" and erases opportunity for engagement. Teams in which all members open up and connect are the most successful.

Another client and government agency did just that. The executive director of a local Illinois park district really took the "engage" part of our process to heart. His style prior to our collaboration was one of stoic sarcasm and cynicism. He understood that he made folks uneasy but was at a loss on how to change.

After our first workshop, where we challenged everyone in the organization to look at how they interacted with each other as a litmus test for how they treated the people they served, this executive director immediately recognized how his style was inhibiting true connections with his team. He also recognized how his lack of connection was trickling down through the organization.

Another potential client of ours also recognized how a lack of sincerity stunts the ability to drive change. During our introductory meeting, as we discussed the methodology that Relationships Matter Now uses to implement concrete and consistent changes in the organizations we serve, the CEO of a privately held local company had a light bulb moment.

As he described all the investments he and his senior team had been making to improve their culture, he stopped and said this out loud: "It just occurred to me when you said what you said about engaging the team, that perhaps me and my partner are part of the reason we cannot move our culture forward."

He went on to describe how his own behaviors and reactions to all the efforts the team was making to change the culture were essentially stunting the company's ability to adopt the change. I am certain that revelation alone is one of the reasons we have yet to work together. He recognized that his own commitment to change was not quite in motion.

The other major barrier to true engagement is lack of skills to extract it. Have you ever been in a brainstorming session where everything you said was met with a negative reaction or ignored? I have, and there is nothing more frustrating than that. Being asked to engage but not having the right leader with the right skill set to cultivate engaging discussions is worse than not attempting to engage at all. While a professional facilitator is the best and preferred option, we realize not all organizations have the budget to hire facilitators consistently. The following tips can help build the skills to drive engaging discussion to connect teams and their goals:

1. Set Aside Ample Time for Discussion

Lack of time for all participants to engage is the number one reason people clam up. Be extremely diligent on giving fair amounts of time for answers in advance. Watch for and control discussion vampires who suck time and the life out of everyone. Allow at least two to three minutes of discussion time for every person participating, and allow yourself as facilitator five minutes of wrap-up and transition time from topic to topic.

2. Conduct Discussion in an Unfamiliar Location

People are creatures of habit. If you conduct a meeting where you want new ideas in a place that is familiar or where you regularly conduct meetings, don't expect much more creativity than you normally get. Taking people out of their comfort zone and making them physically and environmentally uncomfortable is one of the best ways to drive connection and engagement. It is preferable to go off-site, but if that cannot happen, make the location as far from familiar surroundings as possible.

3. Have Specific Goals for the Discussion

Create very specific goals for your discussion. Tell the group what you desire to occur in the meeting. Make it clear what you are aiming for, and set an agenda. The more prescriptive you are in advance, the more likely your participants will come ready to work.

4. Create Familiarity and Focus with an Icebreaking Activity

This activity can be used to team build and help drive understanding. Think about our definition of engage - we want bonding to the topic/idea. People have to bond together first to be able to bond as group to the idea you wish to drive. Sometimes people use random icebreaking games, but I like to ensure that they somehow also focus on the task at hand. For example, if I am asking a group to learn how to collaborate more and expecting them to collaborate as part of our discussion, then I'm going to pick an icebreaking activity that requires some quick collaboration.

5. Respect

Respect is the most important aspect of driving engaging discussions. Respect for time. Respect for people. Do not allow disrespect of any kind during your facilitated discussion. Move through topics as close to the announced timeframes as possible. Move people along in their sharing; do not allow one person to dominate the discussion. Attempt to draw out people who seem shy, but respect their responses. Do not shame anyone for his or her over- or underparticipation. Keep the discussions lighthearted, even when the topics move in heavy directions. The energy in the room determines the level of engagement you get. Keeping a respectable environment drives higher levels of engagement over time.

The final barrier to true engagement is infrequency. We've found that many organizations, especially large ones, have only one way and one time of year that they encourage enterprise-wide engagement. Many smaller organizations, due to their lean nature, have little to no formal means to drive engagement. Much like insincerity and lack of facilitation skills, infrequent opportunities to engage nullify the ability to truly engage associates. Earlier in the chapter, I asked you to think about touch points and ways people currently communicate in your organization. Now, I want you to take time to think about safe spaces in which groups of people are able to engage in goals and pertinent topics.

- Are there formal or informal methods for feedback gathering?
- How often do they occur?
- Who drives those conversations?
- Are we communicating outcomes of those discussions?

We must intentionally create space in our companies for people to participate in activities that encourage engagement. This can often be accomplished within the current touch points you have with associates. Think about regular meetings. Whether they are small department meetings or larger enterprise-wide gatherings like quarterly or town halls, look for and make space for times when people can have engaging discussions. Again, remember how we are defining *engage* - we are looking to help people bond themselves to our content. If we can create opportunities for story-to-story connections during our normal communication and touch points, we have a better chance of all the content "sticking" and driving change and behaviors in our teams.

Engage at Home: More Fulfilling Family Time

Driving action in a family can be as challenging if not *more* challenging than driving any workplace team. I get fatigued even thinking about this after a day of driving my Relationships Matter Now team and hosts of client partners. However, as imperative as Engage, Collaborate, Lead is at work, it may be even more imperative in our personal lives where every interaction matters more.

My family of four implemented my business's definition of engage to transform our annual ten-plus day summer trip to Mexico. Since 2010, when both Barreto kids were in school full-time, we've rarely traveled extensively outside traditional breaks. Our annual family visits to Mexico have always been a highlight and a tough part of our calendar each year. With limited time off, we have been constrained on how much vacation we can actually have each year while juggling a family visit. As anyone can attest, visiting family and vacations are not synonymous, and that does not change because our family is in Mexico. For us, vacations signify hotels, pools, eating out, and excursions, and while we get some of those things on some of our trips to visit family in Mexico, two years ago, we needed to do something different. As the wife and mom of the clan, my job was to plan these visits, and it often fell on me to find the "fun" for us in between the mosquito attacks and other slight discomforts that accompany visiting family in our non-resort town in Morelos. One year, we went to Acapulco, but I ran out of time to look for outings, and we only did day trips to Taxco or Tepotzlán. Think of it as going to New York City for the day when you live in suburban New Jersey - fun, but nothing super fun or memorable.

In 2013, that changed. While planning our twelve-day summer visit that spring, I enlisted the Barreto kids to help us. I sat them down and explained to them that we needed an outing away from Morelos, just us. I admitted that I had little to no time to figure it out and asked if they could help. Giving them only a few parameters - it had to be within driving distance of Abuelita's house (no more than five hours) and something they actually wanted to do. That was it. Not truly believing they would help, I'd secreting thought about looking into hotels on another coast in Guerrero near Acapulco, just in case.

Within two weeks, my oldest came back with a destination. She introduced me to El Árbol de Tule in Oaxaca, one of the oldest living trees in the world. She told us they'd learned about it in class and promptly Googled it to show me why going to Oaxaca on our next trip would work perfectly. Using Google Maps, she showed that while it was close to six hours away versus my five-hour limit, there were so many attractions we could see, including a pyramid: Montalbán. She'd already floated the idea by my husband who had endorsed it and let us know he'd never been to the tree town either. My son joined in on the exploring, and before you knew it, the whole family was engaged in our upcoming trip. I quickly found a quaint hotel with Wi-Fi access, and we were golden.

What's more telling about engaging the whole family in that Mexico visit planning is what happened next. We had a trip to California already planned for spring break, and it was happening two weeks after we'd laid out our plan for Mexico together. Flying into San Francisco and out of Santa Ana, we had ten days of hanging with family and friends in both the Bay Area and Los Angeles County loosely planned. Our son, who was seven at the time, asked us a week later if he could give us an activity for spring break.

Unsure of what exactly he was going to suggest, we hesitantly told him we'd consider it. He proceeded to tell us that we should add a stop at Tony's Pizza Napoletana to our San Francisco places to eat. I have never seen him so excited as he pulled up a DVR'd episode of the Travel Channel show *Food Paradise* and showed us the pizza place he referenced. He went on for a few minutes about what pizza we should try and pretty much made us agree on the spot.

Not only was it fantastic pizza and a great way to end our day of sightseeing in Chinatown in San Francisco, it awakened our children's interest in contributing to our activities while we traveled. Travel is a huge family value in the Barreto household. We cherish every opportunity we have to explore new cities and lands. By implementing engagement - to bond (as oneself) to do something - in our family that one time for a Mexico outing out of frustration, every trip since then, a Barreto child has stepped up to lead on an aspect of our travel itinerary. What an amazing and rewarding way to build memories together! I can also add that there are fewer conflicts on these trips now. You can genuinely see that every member of the family has contributed to our desired outcome, and it makes for peaceful, fulfilling time away from home.

Further, each person has connected something important to him or her to the greater story our family is building. Now as I begin the process of planning time away from home, there is so much less pressure on me. The entire clan weighs in and bonds itself to ensure that we have an enjoyable new adventure each time we set foot outside of Illinois.

Think about ways you may use our definition of engage in your life outside work - perhaps with that community group you volunteer with or as you are mentoring someone with the Boys & Girls Clubs. Remember, to drive outcomes where people are invested fully, you need to engage them and connect their story to the greater story.

Chapter One in Review: ENGAGE

1. Define Engage
   a. Hottest buzzword of the new century
   b. Focus on our definition: to bond (as oneself) to do something
2. Why Engage
   a. How adults learn
   b. Beyond the brainstorm
   c. Engagement drives mobilization
3. Barriers to True Engagement
   a. Insincerity of leadership
   b. Lack of skills to extract engagement
   c. Infrequency of engagement opportunities
4. Five Tips to Facilitating Engaging Discussions
5. Engage in Your Personal Life

Chapter One: ENGAGE Notes

2
COLLABORATE

Getting people engaged is truly the toughest part of the Engage, Collaborate, Lead method of change. Once people are engaged, the next piece of the puzzle is almost intuitive. However, as with *engage*, there has been a heightened use of the word *collaborate* and its derivatives since the start of the twenty-first century.

The origins of the word are matched up with our present-day use:

LATIN
col-
together
            Collaborare ⟶ *Collaborat*
LATIN
laborare   *worked with*
to work

Here are definitions of the verb *collaborate* from *Merriam-Webster*:

1. to work with another person or group in order to achieve or do something
2. to work jointly with others or together, especially an intellectual endeavor
3. to cooperate or willingly assist an enemy of one's country and especially an occupying force
4. to cooperate with an agency or instrumentality with which one is not immediately connected.

At first glance, these definitions do not all align with the spirit in which Relationships Matter Now uses the word. Founded by a marketer, our company looks at *collaborate* more along the lines related to definition number one—"working in order to achieve or do something"—and we even interchange *collaborate* with a marketing term, *cocreate*. We will interchange the terms collaborate and cocreate throughout our discussion. We gravitate toward cocreate because it is such a valued strategic marketing term.

BusinessDictionary.com defines cocreation as "a business strategy focusing on customer experience and interactive relationships. Cocreation allows and encourages a more active involvement from the customer to create a value rich experience."

Over the last four years, however, we have seen *collaborate* play out more like a combination of the *Merriam-Webster* fourth definition and the business definition of *cocreation*. Think about your current organization. Aren't there warring factions of people who often see one another as competition or the enemy? My mind immediately goes back to my days as a corporate marketer. The sales group was the nemesis of our marketing team. In retail, it played out as buyers or merchandisers versus marketing or buyers versus inventory. Some of the commotion was self-fulfilling based on our own feelings, but some of it was the responsibility of our leaders. In one organization, the sales team was called revenue generating while marketing and accounting were called non–revenue generating in open meetings by senior leaders. It's no wonder there was bad blood between the departments. And we see that today with many of our government agency clients. When bringing groups together for strategic planning sessions, you can see the factions—police versus public works, public works versus parks and recreation, and of course, administration versus everyone else. This reflection on the climate in many organizations leads me to see collaboration as the feat of getting "cooperation between agencies where there is no apparent connection."

Understanding the definitions and origins of collaboration is the main reason Relationships Matter Now seeks to engage people first. We engage people to make the emotional connection where there is not a visible, tangible one. Only then can you move toward collaboration in the true sense of its original Latin meaning -"work together with."

Collaboration has never been more prevalent in everyday life at any other time in history as it is today, thanks in part to social media. We used to see one-way communication in all areas, all sectors, and across industries - linear and limited communication sent in one direction to persuade or command. Gone are the days where one-way communication ruled. Today, and since the beginning of this new century, we've evolved to understand that interaction is king.

Collaborate (or *collaboration*) is an even stronger buzzword in the new century with mentions in over 4,500 nonfiction book titles written since 2001—over 48 percent more than books with the word *engage*. And while business is still the lead genre with over 24 percent of the book titles, *collaborate* shows up in politics and education-related titles at a 20 percent higher rate than *engage*. Everyone recognizes the importance of collaboration, but few know how to execute the technique to get the desired results. In fact, the result is the first place to start when looking to collaborate with multiple parties.

The Result

The key to effective collaboration and cocreation is alignment with the end result. It has to be crystal clear what the ultimate goal is before your begin the process of moving toward it. This is the number one reason we have gridlock in federal government. There is never alignment with the ultimate goal. On paper, everyone says they are aligned, but were that true, they would align and cocreate the solutions to many of our persistent problems. We do it on a local government level every day.

Relationships Matter Now has a local government client that, at first, appeared to have no hope of doing anything, anytime soon. When we started our engagement, the disjointed elected board of officials were frustrated with each other and were not focused on where the municipality was headed. There were no imminent financial issues or visible controversies, but they just could not come together on any item put before them to vote. This dynamic had their staff on eggshells, and they were essentially lost as to what was expected of them from their policy leaders.

One of their officials saw me speak at the annual Illinois Municipal League conference, where all Illinois elected local officials and staff congregate for best practice exchange and professional and organizational development opportunities. My session particularly struck a nerve with this official because of the direct nature by which I focused on public service and the importance of having a plan. He invited me to a board meeting within ninety days of our meeting, and it was then that I saw the challenge ahead. We built a rapport with the entire board, albeit a cool and distant one. And over the next few months, Relationships Matter Now pulled each official into the greater story of the municipality to ensure that all parties were engaged. During this phase, we had an official declare that he did not intend to run for reelection. This is very common in the engage and collaborate stages of our practice. We appealed to his current responsibility to residents to keep him engaged enough to move us as a group to collaboration. We will address self-selected attrition later in this chapter, but understand that setting the stage for fruitful collaboration starts with engagement and alignment with the ultimate goal.

Our crew of officials in this small municipality just across the Wisconsin state line and over sixty miles from Chicago were far apart philosophically as we began our work session on their plan. You could cut the tension in the room as we discussed the SWOT analysis data. It was clear where allegiances in the room lay. Short, curt vocal tones and body language made it clear this group was ready to fight. As we dissected the data from both their business and residential community (among the highest response rates I'd ever seen in all my years of cold-data collection), it was clear what priorities their constituents felt were necessary.

We spent at least ninety minutes going over this, and finally it occurred to me that this group did not understand their purpose as policy leaders. It is not written anywhere that agreement must occur in order to take action. Just on a hunch, I polled the room to see who'd used the word *alignment* in recent years. Very few folks raised their hand. We quickly pulled up alignment on the iPad and spent five minutes talking about why alignment was actually what we were going for versus agreement.

I have never seen so many people instantly relieved of pressure in one place, at one time. Alignment with the goal changed our energy in the room for the better immediately. Seven months later, at the next IML annual conference, the leader of that municipal board told the story of aligning with what needed to be done and how it changed the team's course for the entire work session. He even used the word *team*, something I had not ever heard him use in the lead-up to our project.

When you are embarking on a goal, it is imperative to get all parties to align with the result you want. Aligning is not agreeing. Aligning is recognizing that adjustments can and will be made to the final result. Aligning also allows for the coordination of positions on an issue. This is the part where you take pieces of what each party wants and find a way to make it work toward the end result. In organizations, this should be rather easy. Profitability and service or product delivery have to top most organizations' list of priorities. While this is rather easy on the government and nonprofit agency side of our business, Relationships Matter Now finds this to be much more challenging in the corporate sector. It should not be, but let's face it, with most corporations no longer managing in clear, direct lines of accountability and structure, we have an uphill battle when faced with driving collaboration in today's corporate environment. Thanks to matrix management, getting all parties to the table for collaboration should actually be easier now than it was when I entered the marketplace in 1993 when this style of management was in its early years of expansion.

Matrix management groups employees by both function and product/service with the desire to combine the best of both structures. This line of thinking matches well with our view of how to collaborate, and because matrix teams have a clear goal, executing cocreation activities should yield great results. Our experience with corporate clients shows us that this works only when we gain the alignment of the project lead or manager.

Not the project lead or manager in your area of influence? Here are three tips to jump-starting a collaboration discussion when you are not the most influential piece of the puzzle.

1. Know the Pain

The result the team is working for is not enough in this case. As an individual contributor or a manager who is not directly responsible for the result, your best course of action is to understand the pain. What keeps the key leader up at night? Relationships Matter Now got a meeting with the world's largest company simply by asking the leader of the division we were targeting what was keeping her up at night. People want to solve the problems behind their pain. Most often, it's on their minds constantly. And even more often, people don't ask. We assume that "that is why they are in that pay grade," and we don't seize the opportunity to step up and shine. Ask the leader of an area or business unit you want to impact what their pain is. You cannot get to the result without this information.

2. Speak Their Language

Even if you understand what keeps them up at night, pay close attention to the language a leader uses. Not only is it a clue to what is important to them, it is also a cue to you on how to influence them. People like their own words or thoughts, which is why it's often not difficult to get opinions. Understanding the language that moves people is a key to getting your ideas heard, especially when you want to gain alignment. Repeat what a leader says and write it down on paper. No offense to digital tablets, but we retain information at a higher rate when we physically write it out. Recently, I had a client who loved to use a phrase she made up as it relates to diversity and inclusion. While the phrase is catchy, I was having a tough time recalling it, so I made a point to record it in a paper notebook the next time we were together. At our next meeting, I found a way to work the phrase into my proposed solution for their strategy we were revamping. You could see the conversion all over her face. Now, this was not a fake or falsified use of her word. I genuinely put together a proposal that could match up to her expectation of delivery and used her own language to make her decision easy. Observe and note language of leaders you want to sway.

3. Offer to Lead or Supply the Leader of the Discussion

This is the most important of the three tips. If you know the pain and believe collaborating on the solution is best, and you've spoken their language to keep discussions alive, getting the discussion scheduled is your last goal. You need a leader of the discussion. You learned how to prepare to lead a discussion in the last chapter, so if you are confident in your skills, you need to step up and lead this discussion. One of the biggest deterrents to ideation for new projects is human resources. We hear all the time that people would rather keep a good idea under wraps until they know there will be resources to execute it. A collaborate or cocreation discussion is no different. You will have an easier time getting your leader on board if you already self-identified to lead it. If you don't have the skills or desire to lead it, then you must have a discussion leader identified before you "make the ask". Again, when putting yourself in that leader's shoes, you have to have already figured out a way to overcome any barriers that will keep you from moving forward with your plan. Look around your team or at other internal teams to see if there are eligible, willing facilitators to lead the discussion. Please note that if the subject matter of the discussion is one in which you want to have input, then do not volunteer to facilitate the discussion. Your best contribution will not be received if you are the overall discussion leader as it would be your job to extract information from all parties and objectively aggregate it. Remember that as well if you are looking for internal facilitators; they need to be neutral on the topic at hand. And finally, if you are looking at external facilitators, be sure to have ideas for funding before you approach the leader. Remember, your job is to bring forth a solution, and you have to account for all the details to demonstrate your empathy for the leader. It also showcases why you are ready to lead.

Once it's clear that people are on board for collaboration, and the result to which you are collectively marching is in alignment, data is your next obstacle.

Data: The Second Most Important Input to Collaboration

Yes, that's right: data is the second most important input in executing good collaboration. The engaged team of people enlisted to collaborate is first, and data is close behind. Very few decisions are made these days in any organization without a set of data points to guide those verdicts. And thanks to the Google revolution, any and every thing that can be measured is measured. Now, not all data is pertinent to collaborate well, and that is the first job of a person driving to execute our proven technique.

Prioritization of data is a strenuous and necessary task to ensure collaboration, and the resulting action is relevant. Currently, many of our clients are nonprofit and government agencies, and their task of data gathering can be tough simply because of the lack of data measured. When there are shortages of data, it is critical to establish baselines or create data points to gather for future measurement.

We have a client who had never gathered any input from its employees in the fifteen-year tenure of the supervisor we were partnering with on our project to improve their culture. As it is a government agency, it did not naturally occur to them that we needed to establish our baseline on what employees currently thought about the culture before we set out to change or improve it. This is not uncommon. We can be so wrapped up in executing our daily tasks and running our businesses that we forget to gather data to ensure that what we are doing is working. This goes beyond what the balance sheet says. A business could be very profitable but at a very high cost due to inefficiencies. This is why we need both qualitative and quantitative data at our disposal to drive change. Let's look at the definition of both:

- *Quantitative data* is information about quantities that can be measured in numbers. Quantitative data tends to be objective in nature and is very precise in measurement.

- *Qualitative data* generates nonnumerical data points and is primarily subjective as it seeks to understand human behavior and reasons that govern behavior.

Clearly, most businesses have some form of quantitative data as that type of data is what drives accounting and IT departments in most all organizations. We assert that quantitative data alone is not enough to drive changes in human behavior in organizations. Think for a moment about the importance numbers have on you personally. These days, we all have access to our precise bank account balance. This enlightened state has impacted the ability of banks to drive revenue from overdraft fees - so much so that *Time* magazine declared in the spring of 2014 that "America's Most-Hated Bank Fee Is on Its Death Bed," citing a fourteen-year-low in revenue generated from this fee.

That is an instance of numbers impacting human behavior in a big way: the fourteen-year low and consecutive drop in fees paid matched exactly with the growth in online and mobile banking. When we know the numbers, we act differently. Companies and organizations do not fare as well. Research shows that the average worker, even upon hearing regular, detailed financial status reports of his or her company, does not understand his or her impact on those numbers. While most of us can understand and connect action to our own personal numbers, that comprehension does not translate to our places of business.

Hence, the addition of qualitative data to supplement the quantitative in most organizational settings is important. Today, when a company is being evaluated for its initial public offering value, no longer are the numbers and financials the only important items. Qualitative elements that make up the company's story can be as powerful—if not more powerful—than its revenue projections and financials. "The story" of the company you work for is often found in the qualitative data that you are not gathering.

Back to that client, it was a government parks and recreation agency that had never gathered any input from its employees. When we began our Journey to Service Excellence (Relationships Matter Now's unofficial name for our parks and recreation custom culture-building program) with this agency, we set out to measure how people understood their roles within the agency before, during, and after our project. We are delighted to report that our efforts had a positive impact on employee perception year-over-year for three consecutive years. Additionally, we saw this client build and secure community support for a tax referendum to expand services for acquired property and facilities that had previously failed in the past. While we cannot take 100 percent credit for the win, we are certain the renewed engagement and cocreation of service-excellence values that could drive performance played a role in driving this initiative across the goal line.

Understanding how your organization's quantitative data (the balance sheet) and qualitative data interact is key to co-creating solutions for your organization. Your desired results or outcomes of your collaboration drive what inputs are necessary. As a rule of thumb, you need to have qualitative input from any group that is affected by the work you intend to execute. Stop and think for a moment who you may be desiring to impact or influence with your final result.

- Is it community members?
- Is it customers of your product or service?
- Who will ensure this happens? Are they at the table?
- What key leaders have a direct impact on the process we are improving?
- How will this touch the frontline employee?

You have to answer these questions before you ever move to get in a room with stakeholders to cocreate or collaborate on a solution. The numbers and the information that impacts the numbers must be gathered and distributed to all parties in advance of your planned work session. With the data and the engaged team of individual stakeholders, you are ready to conduct your work session.

Four Keys to an Actionable Cocreation Session

1. Break Data into Sound Bites

Busy people love sound bites. In our current twenty-four-hour news cycle that is on steroids with social media input by the minute, most adults are used to sound bites. Originally a term for broadcast media that meant a short, recorded extract that was chosen for its pungency or appropriateness, *sound bite* has come to mean "a brief catchy comment or saying." For our purposes, think of short, summarized, pertinent points. Create a sound bite sheet of the most important data points from the overall data set. This will be time-consuming for you but will save the team valuable work time together. Summarize repeated points and note the instances they were mentioned. There is significance in that information.

It is important that all parties who will participate in a cocreation work session have access to the complete data set in advance. You want to be sure the process is as transparent as possible. However, we also know and understand the human tendency to skim or scan long documents. By providing the sound bite sheet, you save time and energy for the rest of the session.

2. Dive into Difficult Conversations

Never avoid the tough topics. This is one of the highest priorities on your work-session productivity list, especially if the difficult topic was broached in the data. Recently, while working with a nonprofit agency going through major changes, we were faced with an inconvenient truth. All members (except one) of our strategic planning qualitative data set pointed out a problem with the commitment of the board of directors. Seventeen out of eighteen respondents to an anonymously submitted SWOT analysis survey cited low board commitments in their written comments. As groups prioritized topics to address, the board commitment was never discussed. After four hours of work, the Relationships Matter Now facilitator raised the issue. Not one person, board or staff, was willing to have the discussion. Chalking it up to the last sunny, warm day of fall in Chicago, the facilitator let the group off—for that moment.

Not only did she record the omission in the discussion in the follow-up notes, but she also put the group on notice that they were going to discuss it to start the next work session while everything was fresh in mind. The next session started with a fifteen-minute discussion that she came prepared for with specific, verbatim quotes from the SWOT data as well as questions to stimulate the group to open up.

Tough conversations cannot be avoided, and here's why:

That tough discussion your organization is avoiding holds the key to the door that opens to where they want the team to go.

Make no mistake: whatever is festering beneath the surface is impacting performance in a major way. This is the organizational cancer effect. How often can you actually see cancer in a cancer patient? Almost never, right? The same principle applies to cancer in organizations, rarely do you see it.

The "organizational cancer" is counting on this lack of visibility to keep growing in a dark, damp spot. Cancers come in all forms. They are specific policies or procedures we won't let go of that hurt our ability to serve one another or our customer well. Cancers can be specific people who leave bodies in the wake of their work, and they can be systemic problems that we don't discuss because they are too hard and require too much to heal.

Do not give cancer any space in your organization. You will never get where you want to go by avoiding tough discussions. This alone is one reason to hire a professional, objective facilitator. He or she will have no interest but to get you through the discussion. In fact, you must ask the facilitator how many of these types of tough discussion they've facilitated to know if they would be willing and capable to guide your organization through a critical conversation.

3. Prioritize, Prioritize, Prioritize

There is never a lack of work to be done in most organizations we encounter. This is especially true of groups trying to move the needle or change direction. In addition to day-to-day work, we have to find ways to incorporate the new and improved processes or solutions a cocreation work session will generate. For this reason, prioritization is key. If everything is important, then nothing is important. The best way to focus your time and energy is to gain the alignment of the entire group around what's most important and when. The data will give you some clues to this, but also take note of the resources—both human and otherwise.

The number one reason most plans fail is a lack of prioritizing correctly. This is the point in the process where you delineate what we "want to do" versus what "we need to do," with all parties involved present. With every stakeholder at the table, it is the best time to gage commitment from the group about the ultimate result we've already aligned with at this point. You force public acknowledgement among the stakeholders of what is critical and what it is not.

As a professional facilitator, this is my worst moment of the entire process. After we've collectively worked hard to interpret the data and rolled up our sleeves to brainstorm solutions, this is the time that hurts most—the moment when we have to leave some of those solutions behind, even if only temporarily. Two big things to keep in mind when prioritizing are that first, you don't have to lose all the new ideas. Review them for feasibility and impact and keep the ones that hit both within your designated work period and save the ones you may use later. Keep a copy of those notes and review them six, twelve, and eighteen months into your execution phase. You never know how the organizational changes can impact your ability to do something now versus a year ago when you and your team first thought of it. Finally, as you prioritize and start to dedicate resources to the final initiatives and tactics, start to crystalize who will make sure these actions happen.

4. Assign Ownership

Every action your group decides is important enough to include in the final plan must have an owner. It is key to make sure that owners of activities have both the talent and financial resources needed to execute assigned tasks. Credibility of the outcome rests on this portion of the work session. People in an organization know the intricacies well, and when we set out with unrealistic action items and owners, we doom our plan to failure. Can you think of a time when you participated in a planning session that laid out all the wrong leaders on all the wrong tasks? Did you believe it would happen? Neither will your people. Make a point to outline gaps you have in talent as you look for fulfill priorities—lack of ownership can be the deciding factor that makes a priority stay on the list or drop off in this planning cycle. The place where this is the hardest to apply is in corporate settings where there are often lots of partial resources. Many times there are plenty of people, but most often, they are stretched to capacity. Unlike their nonprofit or government counterparts, who are just short on headcount, corporate entities often have human resources that are fragmented across businesses and functions. This is the time to take your senior leader up on the offer of "let me know if there is anything I can do." Every person reading this has heard that phrase from a senior leader in the company and never cashed that favor in. Now is the time. Human resource obstacles are what leaders at higher pay grades are compensated to remove. It's on you to inform them of the exact needs so that they can act.

With the correct resources in place and clear ownership of initiatives and tactics created, you have succeed in executing the final step in a fruitful collaboration exercise.

The final look out of this phase of the Engage, Collaborate, Lead methodology is the blessing and curse of self-selection.

Self-Selection: The Attrition Factor You Had Not Anticipated

Relationships Matter Now has used its Engage, Collaborate, Lead technique on more than seventy projects across thirty-eight unique clients, and every time, we have experienced an attrition factor that only our team anticipates in advance: self-selection. Be it frontline staff, middle managers, or appointed or elected board members, we always have people self-select out of an organization during our project or shortly afterward.

This is an unintended but positive side effect of executing Engage, Collaborate, Lead in your organization. I remember vividly the very first time it occurred in a parks and recreation agency, where we were reshaping the culture by co-creating and implementing custom service-excellence values for this suburban Chicago government body.

We started our journey with a series of facilitated discussions on customer service and service excellence delivery. One particular middle manager was sour on the concept from the start. Not only did her body language tell me she was not going to be engaged, but every verbal contribution to our discussion made her intentional disconnection from the group more apparent. She slumped in her chair from the moment the workshop started. She rolled her eyes and tried to conduct side conversations that I immediately squashed at every opportunity.

When it was clear that we expected her to contribute—especially because she had a team reporting to her—she looked at me defiantly and said, "It does not matter what you say, people are people, and they are gonna do what they have to do to do their jobs." She closed her comments with a smirk, as if she were daring me to cross her. And cross her I did.

"We are building values today that we all can act on that help us execute our jobs even better than we currently do." I replied to her sternly and noticed how many people in the room perked up and tuned in to our exchange.

It was clear in that moment that the organization was taking a stand: a stand to build and honor values that everyone had input to create. While there was no more interaction, it was clear that my swift and short reply to her had set a new tone. Before that, most people were participating in the discussion but tempering their thoughts and looking toward that manager for unspoken approval of what they were saying. She did not give it, so you could see they were impacted by her presence and attitude. After our exchange, I made a point to review questions and comments that we'd discussion pre-dustup and got much more response from the team.

As you can imagine, that exchange that day was the beginning of the end for that middle manager. After the event, frontline employees and senior leaders alike took time to thank me for "standing up" to "Amy." I was puzzled by their thanks and kept it in mind for our next meeting one year later.

When we reconvened, you could see a different disposition from the entire staff. Not only was it visible in their interactions with each other and the Relationships Matter Now facilitator, it was also evident in their survey answers about the environment versus the prior year. Amy was still in the room, but you could see that her influence had declined. Her disengagement was ignored, and our session was more productive than the previous year. As we closed the session, I commended the group on their growth toward building an environment that delivers excellence to their customers consistently. Further, I implored to them to step it up and drive their new values deeper into the fabric of their service delivery.

They responded and stepped up to the point that middle manager, eighteen-year veteran, and frontline team leader Amy decided she could no longer work in the agency. She imploded under the pressure of delivering excellent service consistently and quit one day out of the blue, giving a mere three days' notice. Managers and frontline team members alike were relieved to see her go, but some people were puzzled by her departure, and the next time I saw them at booster training, Amy's meltdown was addressed.

"It's really quite simple. You guys merely followed through on the promise you made together to deliver great service internally to one another and to your guests, and Amy simply could not step up." This was my response to someone's mixed feelings about losing such a long-standing employee.

Self-selection happens when you effectively take steps to move the enterprise from where it is to where you want it to be. It becomes painfully clear to people who are not aligned with your new direction that they are no longer welcome. You start to build an environment that does not tolerate apathy toward the goal. Ironically, it's never a surprise to anyone in the company who is paying attention.

Associates know the people in their organization who need to be corrected or coached out, but rarely are these offenders addressed directly. These people are also part of the organizational cancer effect we discussed before. More often than not, they are a known distraction, and management simply has not mustered the energy or courage to handle them. Besides, it can seem extremely subjective to address a poor performer head on without a specific framework or plan of action for the offending parties. That is why we address this topic at this point in the Engage, Collaborate, Lead journey. Once you have the members of your team engaged and begin to address challenges head on and cocreate frameworks and tactics for solving them, people or processes that don't fit your new direction tend to fall away.

We see this on appointed boards all the time. When a nonprofit agency builds clarity on direction and lays out initiatives that need action, board members who don't fit or agree often walk away. Many nonprofits panic when this happens, and we assure them that by focusing on what they want in a board member, they will only suffer temporarily the loss of an ineffective one.

One of our small nonprofit boards saw this firsthand. A small local branch of a national nonprofit went through a rigorous strategic planning process in 2011 with us. After surveying both their funders and the grantees the agency funded, we tackled the SWOT analysis of both the staff and board. The small board of eight members and a chair had only four active directors alongside four apathetic ones. All board members participated in all the data analysis and in the eight-hour work session. During this meeting, you could see the frustration of the staff and active directors every time an inactive member spoke. As a facilitator, it was tough to manage the bad blood that kept creeping up in our group work discussions, but alas, we completed our framework and started to assign ownership.

Right in the middle of this exercise, one board member got up and declared that he no longer wanted to serve and was resigning immediately following the work session. Everyone sat shocked at his declaration, yet the board chair thanked him for his candor and asked that the group press on to finish the task at hand. That one move signaled to the group that we were committed on our direction and would press on with or without said board member. Not only did this embolden the board, but it also rejuvenated the staff in the work session and carried us to the completion of the initial strategic planning framework.

The executive director later shared that two additional board members resigned within six months of adopting the new strategic plan. And while it was difficult during the first four months, they quickly recruited one enthusiastic board member and plugged him into several strategic initiatives.

"Having our plan and being able to articulate the direction we were going opened up a conversation with a volunteer who we'd never considered to ask to join the board. He asked us if there were any openings, and we were able to plug him right in," stated the executive director enthusiastically at our twelve-month coaching checkup.

Self-selection was a curse to her organization in the short term but provided a better long-term blessing of converting an active volunteer to a new, engaged board member. Know going into your Engage, Collaborate, Lead process that you will invariably lose people who are not willing to go where you are taking your organization. Understanding and making peace with this possibility will save you unnecessary stress when and if it happens to you.

Take a few moments to reflect on people who currently inhibit your organization's ability to move in the direction you and your leadership know it needs to go. Sometimes it's necessary to have a preevent, preemptive "level setting" expectation discussion with a problematic member of the team. It is very simple to lay out why the company is embarking on the journey, what the team hopes to accomplish, and be direct with what is needed from that specific team member. By doing so, you set the stage for what's to come and give the troubled party a chance to evaluate where they see themselves in the impending process. Most often, they either get on board and have a renewed interest in participating, or they make plans to exit.

Either way, the entity benefits, and the path is clear to foster the final stage of enabling all team members to lead moving forward.

Collaborate outside Work

By now, you have seen how the collaborate piece of our equation works in work environments across industries and work levels. It is equally effective in other endeavors outside the office. One of the places I've seen this work magically is in my volunteer work. Whether it is a nonprofit board that I serve on or my church youth committee, taking the time to engage people to cocreate direction leads to greater achievement of overall objectives. It even works in youth-coaching environments.

For three years, I was drafted by my daughter to lead a youth worship team at our megachurch in suburban Chicago. I say drafted because while I am always willing to lend my talents to places in need—and especially entities that serve me and my family—dealing with other people's kids is one of my least favorite activities. I am convinced that the toughest part of my job as a parent is dealing other parents, their children, and their influence on my children and environments. So when my daughter asked me with her big, brown, begging eyes to be a leader for the fourth-through sixth-grade worship team she'd just won a spot on, I begrudgingly obliged. I regretted the decision almost immediately and every week until our third month of service.

Our main duties were to lead worship for other children in preschool through kindergarten and first grade classrooms. In addition to learning the songs, we had to learn motions and guide the young children through the two to four songs each time we served. This duty was only one-fourth of the time we had together each time we served. The other three-fourths required me to occupy them until the service was over and their parents picked them up. Did I mention that we had three church services over two weekend days? So over the course of the weekend, it was 145 minutes with my kid plus four others her age with little to no structural guidance from our volunteer leaders. Very quickly, I was looking for ways to find a substitute and bow out. This commitment happened simultaneously as I was starting my company and leaving my corporate full-time marketing role. I was sure I'd get too busy and not feel guilty about bailing until one weekend in December.

After trying and trying to compete with gadgets and the disparate interests of my group, which consisted of two fifth-grade boys and three fourth-grade girls, it occurred to me one day that the only thing that connected us was our team name that we'd creatively come up with the first night at our orientation workshop. I remembered how that night, with that activity, every child in my group was engaged and excited to participate. Channeling the good vibes we'd built that night, I decided to hold a brainstorm session with my team, the Disco Donuts, to decide what we would do with all our time together each service weekend.

At first, you could see that each child was somewhat disconnected from the objective—how to best use all the extra time in between performances. Why? They'd been running around doing whatever they wanted during those torturous 145 minutes each weekend, so why would they want to change that? Right away, I had to convince them there was an issue and that I needed their help solving it. Second, I needed to engage them again and connect them to our story—the story of the Disco Donuts. We gave each other nicknames and built a value of bringing a snack item each time we served together.

From there, we also created a "safe space" time to chat about what was going on in our lives and how we wanted our team to pray for us in the coming week. Finally, we allowed a gadget time to play on electronic devices for a specified twenty minutes each weekend as well as a card and/or board game slot where we all played together. Before long, we laid out a framework for how we'd spend our 145 minutes each service weekend. I'm happy to say that we never had any issues or complaints about boredom for the rest of that year. And the next two years, I repeated the same process with our new team as we rotated in new members. Not only was it a hit for our team, but I shared the framework with other leaders and saw them implement similar brainstorm sessions and custom schedules for their own groups. Before I stopped volunteering in youth ministry altogether as my company grew, I used that framework to train other youth ministry volunteer leaders in the drama and music area of our church's volunteer organization.

The nine-to-eleven-year-olds in that church group were not much different from the adults I was dealing with in my new business. Enabling them to tie themselves to a story greater than themselves was the first step to moving them toward true leadership. Helping those kids understand that occupying their time well between performances helped their fifteen-minute time onstage leading younger children in worship and made it easy for them to take ownership in laying out our schedule. Surely, I could have dictated how we would spend our offstage time together, but I am certain we would not have had the impact we had on our team and beyond.

People have an innate desire to contribute and often just need the right leaders to extract their contribution. In settings like churches or nonprofit volunteer organizations, it is easy to drive forward with what we'd like to do to make our own service experience go more smoothly without ever enlisting the thoughts, ideas, and effort from the greater group. However, when thinking about the experience of everyone and the goals of the organization you are serving, it is best to cocreate solutions for challenges. Our work with those young worship leaders not only enhanced their service experiences as volunteers, but we better focused them to deliver great worship experiences to the younger students they were leading each week. Everyone in our story won - the students who volunteered to lead worship, the recipients of their worship talents, and myself and other parent volunteers - simply because I collaborated with two eleven-year-old boys and three girls between the ages of nine and ten to better use their spare time during service weekends.

Think about areas outside of work where you give your time and talents. Reflect on how you can challenge those situations for improvement with the following questions:

- Are we doing our duties in the most efficient way?
- Have we enlisted the ideas of the folks who do this regularly?
- How can we serve _____ better?
- Does our activity support and further our mission?

Once you have your mind starting to think about answers to these questions, be sure to collaborate with your peers on finding the collective answers to those questions. You will see greater movement toward the goals as well as have a richer volunteer experience.

Chapter Two in Review: COLLABORATE

1. Define Collaborate
   a. Origins/definition
   b. Why collaborate
2. Align with the End Result
   a. Alignment versus agreement
   b. Three tips for jump-starting collaboration when you're not in charge
3. Data—Tool for Collaboration
   a. Why data is necessary
   b. Qualitative versus quantitative data and why you need both
   c. Four keys to an actionable cocreation session
4. Self-selection and the unanticipated attrition factor
5. Collaborate outside work

Chapter Two: COLLABORATE Notes

3
LEAD

Now we enter a place in our process that we have been intentionally working toward since we started: bringing about leadership or enabling the ability to lead. Much like our previous words, *leadership* has grown in usage in the twenty-first century.

Unlike *engage* and *collaborate*, *lead* is a bit trickier to define. The transitive verb is defined in *Merriam-Webster* as follows:

1
    a : *to guide on a way especially by going in advance*
    b : *to direct on a course or in a direction*
    c : *to serve as a channel for*
2   *to go through : live*
3
    a (1) *to direct the operations, activity, or performance of*
    (2) *to have charge of (3) to ask (a witness) a question in a way that suggests what the answer should be*

    b (1) *to go at the head of (2) to be first in or among*
       (3) to have a margin over

4 to bring to some conclusion or condition
5 to begin play with
6
    a to aim in front of (a moving object)
    b to pass a ball or puck just in front of (a moving teammate)

Further, when you look closely at its usage in the twenty-first century, you will see a shift in how the world uses both lead and leadership. Since 2001, 39,337 nonfiction books have been written with *lead* in the title: almost one-third of those have been written since 2007, and over 98 percent of them are in the business and management genre. During the same time frame, 85,161 nonfiction books included *leadership* in their title, but 75 percent of those came after 2007. Business and management still lead all categories with close to 72 percent of the titles, but note that 13 percent of all those titles are in the self-improvement or self-help genre—nearly double the percentage at the start of 2001.

This clearly demonstrates that there is an appetite for leading and leadership that is growing, and while it continues to be strong in business and management, the growth of the self-improvement and self-help aspects of leadership points to a new awareness of what it means to lead.

As Relationships Matter Now began its operations, leadership and leadership of self were huge contributors to the formation of Engage, Collaborate, Lead as a value proposition. All my experiences up to the point of articulating the brand promise of my company pointed to a truth: people need to lead. Regardless of where they are in life or career, leading is a necessary component to living well. Humans lead themselves, processes, systems, and sometimes other humans. Since our new century began and especially in the last seven years, it appears that more people are examining what's necessary for leading or leadership.

Defining *lead* for our book really points us back to the definitions laid out before, especially the very first one: to guide on a way; to direct on a course or in a direction; to serve as a channel. We firmly see leadership as guiding and directing but only after there is the investment of engaging and collaborating. Those two previous steps of *engage* and *collaborate* that we have explored deeply point to and create space for the *lead*.

Stop and think back to times in your life when you have felt you were led well. One of my first memories of this was during my first PR internship my senior year of college with an indoor professional soccer team in Chicago. My leader, Steve, the PR and marketing director for the team, was my first example of true leadership from start to finish. I saw immediately in the interview process that he saw my potential service to him as an intern would be a mutual relationship of good. Not only did he budget for a small stipend to cover my expense - something a larger, more lucrative sports team that I simultaneously interviewed with did not do - he was clear on what he intended for me to learn during our time together.

After I accepted the assignment, I saw immediately that he indeed invested in learning about me. He spent hours alongside me making copies in the early days of my work. At the time, I did not even see it for what it was. I remember thinking that he was micromanaging me or that he did not trust me to make simple copies, but in actuality, he was getting to know me before the season started. The few weeks we had leading up to our season was spent getting to know me and engaging me in the history and story of this indoor soccer team. Then, when the season started, he laid out a framework for how he wanted me to work but left flexibility for my input.

There were clear tasks that needed to happen for each game; press releases and stats had to be laid out in advance in the press box. The food for the media had to be ordered and a room assigned for rest before each game. And ensuring all the statistics and fun facts about players were funneled to the overhead announcer throughout the game was among the most important aspects of my job. However, *how* I did these things was left up to me. Steve was clear on what needed to be done but relinquished the method to his young and eager intern.

By the time we were halfway through the season, not only had I mastered delivering all the expected duties, but I'd also enlisted volunteers to help so that I could be free to learn even more from Steve in the final stretch of the season—so much so that he was able to allow me to lead the press box completely while he went on to be mentored in other aspects of team management from the GM. It was a glorious experience and quite honestly ruined me for the early part of my career.

I expected all my managers to lead me as Steve had in that very first experience, and I was sorely disappointed and brought back to earth with my first job at US Soccer. Steve was my first example of Engage, Collaborate, Lead. His careful and precise planning of my orientation to the team and getting to know me well personally gave him the confidence that he could collaborate with me on how to best execute our duties as a team. This eventually led to him enabling me to lead the operations and freed him up for further development. Again, I challenge you now to take a moment to look back at times in your life - personally or professionally - when you were led well.

- Was it clear what was expected of you?
- Would you say your manager "knew" you well?
- Did you have the ability to contribute to your own learning?
- How did you feel when given a chance to lead?

Be sure answer all those questions because if you think of an instance where you cannot answer all those questions, chances are you were not led well in that particular case.

By our definition, leading is guiding and being a beacon for something that is already there. My ability to lead has always been in me, and I have been blessed with leaders throughout my life who took the time to extract and develop that leadership within me. As you seek to lead, there are a few things that need to be in place: clarity, measurability, and flexibility.

Three Criteria to Leading Well

Clarity is the first and most important aspect of leading. What is the goal? Building up to now, we have prepared people to be clear on where we are going by engaging them and collaborating on the objective, and now articulating easily and in a memorable way is imperative. Relationships Matter Now does this in one area of our practice particularly well. In our culture-building and service-excellence training for parks and recreation agencies, we've mastered clarity for our partners.

Across the state of Illinois, Relationships Matter Now has worked with over twenty parks and recreation agencies on transforming their organizational culture through service-excellence training that originates in building custom service-excellence values as a team. We have proven again and again that engaging the entire team to collaborate on a solution for better customer service enables leadership from all team members. The "awesomesauce" in our scalable, repeatable process boils down to the articulation of their custom service values. We always encourage no more than three to five values, and we insist on clear language usage to explain.

This drives clarity. A few words versus many words have a better chance of being remembered and acted upon. Think about TED or TEDx talks and why they are so popular. TED is a global set of conferences owned by the private nonprofit Sapling Foundation, under the slogan: "Ideas Worth Spreading". As I was preparing for my first TEDx talk in 2013, at least eight to ten articles and one e-book all stressed having no more than five points you were trying to get across during the short presentation. People remember things best in small chunks. We have put this concept to test in our parks and recreation agency service-excellence projects.

Team members from my very first project come up to me at the annual state conference and spit back to me their agency's service-excellence values. "Knowledge, empathy, and resourcefulness: I still remember to this day what values we created," said a recreation supervisor from a suburban agency near O'Hare airport. Her declaration was unprompted, and I barely remembered as it was created over four years ago. Yet to her, this was top of mind when she saw me. I'd be willing to bet that she must have seared those words into her heart to recall them years later in a hotel ballroom.

That is the power of relevant language. You see it in marketing campaigns as well. I bet you can name the catchphrases or tag lines for each of the following brands:

Nike
McDonald's
Budweiser
Subway
Gillette

How did you do? I'm sure you knew each of them. Why am I so sure? The combined ad spend on the above brands was over $4.4 billion at the year-end of 2013. All but one of the brands' most recognized tag lines were three words or less:

Just do it
I'm loving it
King of beers
Eat fresh

Executives at the aforementioned brands count on crisp and consistent messaging to influence your behavior. Consistency is an extension of clarity. Your message can be clear and on point, but if you only deliver it once, it will not stick. Further, if you only choose one way to deliver it, it will also lose its effectiveness. Look no further than data on US advertising spend.

Nine different mediums were cited in attributing the $171 billon total US media spend in 2013. And while television continues to lead all categories, the other eight continue to have a strong showing, driving home the point that you have to reach people in many forms with your message. Many people in the United States claim they are not affected by advertising, but it is simply not true. Corporations would not be spending so heavily and intentionally across many mediums to deliver a message they believed was not landing. Think about the forms of media as well.

Advertisers spend another fortune on creating relevant messages for all the containers where potential users will be. Whatever the effort or goal, being able to communicate the idea clearly, concisely, and consistently makes or breaks the desired outcome for that message. Stop for a moment and think about a message you have been trying to convey in your organization.

- Is the message clear?
- Does it quickly hit the most important points?
- Can it be easily repeated?

Those questions cover clarity and need to be addressed first and foremost in any effort of change. Now look at consistency.

- Are my targets getting my message in more than one form?
- Do they get my message more than one time?
- Am I hitting all the senses with my message?

Those questions assist you in delivery of your message steadily over time.

To lead well and to drive behavior and change, the message must be clear. All parties affected directly or loosely - must be able to understand and articulate the goals in order to have any movement toward them. With explicit, succinct, and regular messaging down, clear milestones to measure success must be in place to ensure movement.

As leaders, we are obligated to set measurable occasions for celebration along our journey. That our best definition of milestones in this context. When driving change in an organization, it is imperative that we see our work as a process versus a definitive "stop and start." Taking time along the journey to recognize achievements builds momentum, and momentum is needed to get to our long-term goal. During the collaboration stage, measurable success factors must be laid out and agreed upon by all of the affected parties. Otherwise, the only owner of the milestones will be the person who set them. This is amply clear in corporate environments.

One global client faced the dilemma of unshared milestones that were being achieved but not to their satisfaction. There is a saying that "what is measured gets done." That is very true in corporate entities. However, the degree to which something gets done - the quality of the output - has much to do with who had the input when it was laid out. In the diversity and inclusion recruiting function, every aspect of the candidate's experience was being measured. The number of candidates reached, the number of visits to specific online sites targeted, the number of applicants, the number of interviews, and the number of offers extended and accepted were tracked on specific diverse partnership opportunities. Key stakeholders throughout the company were proud of the numbers, and they were touted on a third-party survey measuring diversity and inclusion across industries. Then in 2013, when one of the surveys updated their methodology and asked additional questions about the recruiting process as it relates to diverse candidates, a shocking narrative came to light. The actual recruiting team, the folks in the field responsible for and accountable to the numbers, had little to no input on how those numbers were laid out. Many team members were just updating the numbers year after year without much due diligence and thought to how they arrived at the goals. They bounced them up the line, got the green light, and kept moving. It was only when the external survey pressed that the organization looked closely to understand the "story behind the numbers," and it was not a pretty one.

Fortunately, this opened a door for greater input into the milestones for diverse candidate recruiting. The numbers alone did not tell the complete story. And isn't that true in life? Let's be real—in today's society, you can find a study or data to support any position. This company learned that looking solely at the numbers is good, but understanding and impacting the story behind the numbers was better. Not only did the company get greater engagement and leadership from their recruiters during this process, but the extra effort was a factor that impacted their ranking on the third-party list and pushed them back into the top spot they lost the previous year. Enlisting recruiters to have more relevant input into the milestones raised their performance in delivery of those milestones. This also applies on a smaller scale.

One of the government agencies we work with set out to change their culture and focus it more on delivering service excellence consistently. As they moved on this path, one of their goals was to raise their community support and drive success on a tax levy referendum. This agency had asked for the levy before, and voters turned it down. As part of their strategic plan, they set out to serve the community better. Specific targets were set for them to understand if they were getting closer to their goal, and every member of the team participated in setting the targets. Along the way, leaders throughout the agency took the time to communicate where they stood in relation to their goals and reinforced the behaviors they wanted to see continue while pointing out those they wished to stop. There were "gut-check" talks along the way on specific goals of internal and external service delivery, and tweaks were made. There were constant connections between the community and the agency on why the milestones laid out were important to everyone. Team members were surveyed, and action was taken to ensure everyone understood their role in achieving the ultimate goal of passing the tax levy referendum. When we say everyone, we mean everyone. From the gal in charge of lawn maintenance to the part-time dance instructor, all people who served residents of this community in any capacity were included on the service-excellence goals and objectives, which included the passing of the referendum.

In the spring of 2013, a full eighteen months after the effort began, this parks and recreation agency gained the financial support of its community to acquire property and expand its recreation efforts through a gradual increase in property taxes over a seven-year period. To be sure you understand the impact, this is in the suburban Chicago area where property values have only slowly begun to stabilize and remain flat after six consecutive years of decline. People in this landlocked community of thirty-seven thousand residents voted to increase their property taxes while their property values were flat after years of decline—all to support their parks and recreation agency's goals to serve them better. This agency carried out Engage, Collaborate, Lead to the letter, and it paid them in spades. All members of their team led this effort, and getting their buy-in early on in terms of milestones was the key driver.

Finally, flexibility is important to leading well. Conditions change. People change. Rigidity is the enemy of innovation. While setting frameworks and structure is important, it is more important to build those frameworks with elasticity. Our favorite example of this is our own company. Founded in 2010 with a focus on relationships and parks and recreation agencies, Relationships Matter Now set out to change the world, one relationship at a time. We built our service offering around wellness and culture building. At the time I started the company, I was still working full-time in corporate America as a marketer for a major US retailer, working more than forty hours a week for them and putting in another thirty to fifty hours a week building my business at night, on weekends, and on vacation time. Plugging along, looking for specific opportunities and strategically placing myself to secure them, it was my flexibility that pushed me out of corporate America for good. Two different marketing projects presented themselves in late 2011. Both came from business colleagues who did not understand what Relationships Matter Now did but knew I was leading it and that I was a marketer.

The calls came within thirty days of each other. One call was to assist in the branding, marketing, and selling of children-focused intellectual property. The owner of the company was based in Atlanta, and after several conversations, I bravely asked to meet in person and booked a ticket to see her the next week. As soon as the trip was booked, I second-guessed myself.

This is not a relationship wellness project, I thought. I tried to convince myself of the good of my hasty decision to go to Atlanta, but it was not working. I was very disheartened that I was headed to a meeting to talk about branding, marketing, and partnership building for this property when my company was all about relationships. Because I set the meeting and had been referred by a friend, I kept the appointment but really had no objective for the meeting. I'd planned to introduce myself and listen to their goals and see where the meeting took me.

The meeting was phenomenal. As the owner of the property showed me the branding, I immediately noted that it was dated. My job at the time was as senior marketing manager for Toys, so I was plugged in to what appealed to kids of all ages. She also struggled to articulate the value proposition of the property, and as I looked at it, I instantly saw how I could articulate the value and bring partners to the table to make this brand a reality. I was charged up. By the time I left the meeting, I was over the moon. The owner of the company drove me to the airport and thanked me for coming down while asking for definitive next steps in our partnership. As I thanked her and left the car, I immediately called the mutual contact who connected us and thanked him for the lead. When I hung up the phone, it was all clear - I was in business. Yes, technically, I had a business for the full year and three months before the trip. However, sitting in that meeting and moving from no objective to full-on sell mode ignited something in me.

    I'd forgotten my malaise about this possible opportunity not being a "relationship" or "wellness" project. It was a *relationship project.* Someone who'd worked with me and trusted me lent their relationship to me to give me a chance at this business opportunity that matched 100 percent with my skills and talents. Further, while sitting in that office in the meeting, talking about all the potential avenues to pursue this intellectual property, I was thinking about all my connections throughout both the toy and entertainment industries - my *relationships*. My relationships that I could activate to move this project forward and bring her property to market. I was calling folks furiously in the days after that Atlanta trip and spent the next thirty days building a team to deliver funding and production possibilities. That project launched me as a business owner, and I cite it today as the first turning point for Relationships Matter Now, and it all hinged on my flexibility to *think* about doing something outside the scope of my original business.

    The second call I mentioned earlier came during those thirty days of euphoria with that initial opportunity. It, too, was a marketing-related project - launching a well-known brand's new retail pints and frozen novelties in grocery chains across the United States. Within another thirty days, I was giving my notice to my employer. The first opportunity fizzled out and never produced one penny of revenue for me. The second deal closed and delivered Relationships Matter Now its first six-figure client in the company's initial eighteen-month existence—all because I took a call to speak to someone about a project outside my predetermined project scope. And I'm glad I learned that lesson early in my entrepreneurial journey. I could write three more identical stories about Relationships Matter Now's pivoting in the marketplace. One of our fastest-growing service offerings today is inclusion and diversity strategy, and I almost did not take "the call" that started it all. When I hesitated, I asked myself the following questions:

- Is this someone who knows me and my talents well?
- If not, were they referred by such a person?
- Do I have the slightest interest in or curiosity about the topic?
- Could I possibly gain a new set of knowledge by engaging?
- What if it's another GGG?

GGG are the initials of that intellectual property that I never got to work on but that tremendously changed my life *anyhow*. Flexibility requires all of the above. Talents and skills can be transferred to other applications. Curiosity and interest drive action. Learning and growth fuel great leaders. Take a few minutes to reflect on how flexible or inflexible you are with yourself and those around you. Great leaders are flexible and are open to flexibility in others. And flexibility is required now more than ever in organizations that operate in a matrix environment.

Three Keys to Leading Well in a Matrixed Organization

Prior to Relationships Matter Now, I spent all my corporate career in three different matrixed organizations: I was with United Airlines, Pella Corporation, and Sears Holding for more than eleven years. It's important to note that the early decade of my career was spent in smaller for-profit and nonprofit environments, so I've seen leadership in all arenas. There is nothing more complex than asserting leadership in a matrix organization. Since the rise of the matrix form of management in the 1970s, there have been questions about its benefits outweighing its disadvantages. Let's quickly define matrix management because sometimes, even if we are living in this form of management, we don't always understand the intention or goals of it. Businessdictionary.com defines a matrix organization as follows:

> *An organizational structure that facilitates the horizontal flow of skills and information. It is used mainly in the management of large projects or product development processes, drawing employees from different functional disciplines for assignment to a team without removing them from their respective positions.*

This often takes the form of business units. As a quick illustration, imagine a large, fictional company that manufactures seven widgets. Instead of having large groups of functional departments, each widget has its own "island of a company" that produces it. Think about Widget A business unit and all functions report to one leader—marketing, production, buying, manufacturing, and any other function. Yet all those functional roles also have reporting accountabilities to functional leaders such as an HR executive or the marketing VP. These are often referred to as dotted-line reports. In this example, you can see that it's somewhat confusing, but you understand the intention to drive ideas and efficiencies around the outcome—the production of Widget A. Regardless of what you do to contribute to the production, you are led by someone whose vested interest is in producing Widget A versus a greater company objective.

The intention of matrix management is to drive deeper accountability to a shared goal across functions. However, in practice, this does not always occur. Like everything else in life, there are too many variables to have a silver bullet management structure that will work under all circumstances. While many companies vacillate between operating in a matrix and not doing so, we have some thoughts on how to lead in an environment where there are lots of players needed to get stuff done.

1. Identify, Build, and Grow Key Stakeholder Relationships

You must pinpoint who the most important players are in your arena to win the game. This seems so simple, but we all know this can be very difficult in large environments. Ask questions. Ask more questions. Look at the paper trail on past achievements. Who was at the table then? Are they still around? Even if someone has moved on from a team, track them down if they are still at the company; chances are, they are still influential in terms of what happens where you sit. Take time to pinpoint all possible people who can impact your work or what you are attempting to execute.

Once you know who the players are, get to know them. Understand their language. What words do they use distinctively from others? Observe what's important to them. I remember building a strong relationship with one influencer of work at Sears Holdings simply by observing and understanding his values. This manager that I had a dotted line to sat in a different building than me. He was tough to nail down for meetings and notorious for triple-booking himself. So even if you got a meeting, chances are he's pushing you off or rushing you because too many people need him. I remember being at my end after my first six months when I noticed one of his rituals. He always took the same path at the same time to eat lunch in the sprawling cafeteria in the atrium area. I could see it from my desk. Whenever I had a pressing question for him that I could not get done over e-mail or get a few minutes of face time in his office, I'd sprint to the stairs to walk to the cafeteria with him. I'd always have my wallet, even if I wasn't going to eat. I got so many projects green-lighted from figuring out his routine for lunch. Then I'd go back to my desk and send him a confirmation e-mail on what we just sealed on the stairs down to lunch, and he'd OK it, every time. Over my four years at Sears, I never had trouble getting storewide marketing's support on any of my efforts for two different business units. Knowing and growing a relationship with key players make all the difference in your outcomes.

2. Manage Downline More Than Upline

This too seems sophomoric to write, but I cannot tell you how often I see people only managing up. Getting your peers and those foot soldiers in the lower levels of your organization on board makes more difference than one senior manager. It's a sheer numbers game, and you must learn to play it. This is also prevalent in our nonprofit agency partner organizations. One middle manager from one of my agency partners had tried for years to get his leadership ignited around customer service and investing in training for part-time and frontline employees, yet year-after-year, no training resources came to him. Finally, early in 2014, he just budgeted on his own and sacrificed dollars from other activities to fund a workshop training with Relationships Matter Now. It was a lean budget, and we did a short, interactive workshop that sparked some life into his part-time team. For three months, they talked about the time together, the exercises we did to team build, and finally the language we agreed to use related to service moving forward. The "buzz" from the legion of close to sixty part-time associates got the attention of some leaders—chiefly the executive director of the organization. We recently sat down to lay out a plan for all team members to partake in service-excellence training. That middle manager effectively managed downline and got all his and his counterparts' direct reports and downline workers to care about customer service. And so instead of continuously begging his boss to do this, he got his team excited about the possible journey to a service-excellence culture, and now we are able to engage senior leaders.

The sheer momentum from figuring out how to manage downline puts a manager in a great position to effect change for two reasons: first, you build a cheering squad. By moving a large number of people on your own, you've demonstrated a key leadership competency of managing influence. Second, you have people who will have your back as you go in to get more resources. Remember the numbers reference a few minutes ago? Going into a leader's office and letting her know that sixty people on her team are already excited about something she never noticed will turn her head immediately, and you have instant credibility on the feasibility of your idea or effort. Managing peers and below can be a key to moving senior leaders.

3. Know Who Makes the Ultimate Decision

There is nothing more important than this point. When you have an idea or concept you want to move forward in a matrix-management environment, it can be downright frustrating to know where the buck stops, but you must know if you plan to accomplish your goals. And sometimes the buck is shared. This is where the two earlier points come in handy again. Think about it. If the decision is jointly made across two areas, knowing the key stakeholders and making great relationships with them can enhance your chances for success. Cross-pollinating (dropping seeds of influence) and understanding impact across functions are necessary. Building momentum across teams also makes sense—imagine going to joint decision-makers and showing you've already got alignment from both sides of the decision-making tree.

Leading well is an organic by-product of engagement and collaboration. Regardless of the environment, leadership is unstoppable when there are connective stories and cocreated solutions that bind a group together.

Enabling Leadership at Home

Very few people who care about leadership intentionally focus on leadership in the family. We take for granted how leadership is expressed and developed outside our work environments. Most folks just go with the flow at home. The topic of leadership outside of work and particularly in families is rarely addressed. Many times birth order and traditional gender roles trump any intentional efforts to foster leadership at home. I'd challenge you to be different.

As a leader of a company and someone who has led almost constantly from a very early age, I find leadership at home to be one of my most challenging areas but a great laboratory for learning. Helping loved ones understand their role in the family and how to best leverage their established and developing talents for the good of the family can make life extremely smooth.

Leaders in the marketplace often abdicate leadership at home, and that is a mistake. And while often times you will play a different role, you need to be as intentional about leadership at home as you are at work. After all, families are the very first communities we serve and use our talents in. Ensuring a positive and encouraging environment that grows talents gives your family members an advantage in their lives outside the family. Over the past three years, we've seen this grow and strengthen our family. Doing a simple personality inventory test has changed the dynamic of our team for the good.

One Sunday afternoon, our preteen daughter took an online personality quiz at http://www.16personalities.com/free-personality-test. It gives a free, robust picture of traits and characteristics across sixteen personality types. She was fascinated at just how accurate the test was and casually asked me to read it to see if I agreed. I am very interested in personality types and have a huge library of books on the topic (on both my physical and digital bookshelves). I decided to temper my excitement and give her the floor, and I did not even share that it was something I knew about. I watched a twelve-year-old growing and developing leader recognize and discover some of her strongest traits for the first time, and it was such an honor. Then I noticed how other members of the family tuned in from across the room: one on his iPad playing a game and the other watching a soccer match while preparing a snack. As we talked more about it, my daughter asked me to take the quiz so that she could see what "type" I was. And even though I'd taken that exact quiz a few weeks earlier on Facebook, I shut my mouth and sat next to her and took it again as if I'd never done it before.

Shortly after that, my results came up, and I was almost the polar opposite of her. As we laughed and compared notes, my eight-year-old son came and joined the discussion with his iPad, asking to take the quiz. Soon we laughed as my son's results revealed that he and I are almost twins—something no one needed a quiz to learn, but we were tickled nonetheless. Finally, my husband joined the party in the family room and camped out with his iPad on the floor in front of the couch. He hesitated but finally agreed to take the quiz. English is not my husband's first language, so we checked to see if he could do it in Spanish. He could not, so we all made ourselves available to him as he did it in English in case he encountered any words that stumped him. We all marveled at his results: they affirmed his twin status with my daughter.

INTP
ISFP
ENFP
ENFJ

The significance of those letters reaches further than their meanings in the personality quiz. Those letters have driven better understanding and communication across our family dynamic every day since that summer Sunday. We understand one another and have more empathy toward each other because of an exercise that many people do in their career and work lives to improve dynamic and work output. Why *not* do that at home? Besides the fun family bonding time we had that day, we equipped our unit to function better together and get better results on what we all work toward. And that changes all the time. Further, I know that the intentional opportunity to develop leadership at home will pay dividends. First, we are growing our children to be self-aware leaders now. My first exposure to understanding my talents fully did not happen until I was a senior in college. Yes, I was twenty years old before I tuned in to my best talents or learned my blind spots. We just gave that exposure to my own kids eight and twelve years earlier, respectively. It also benefitted my husband, who grew up in central Mexico and who had never done anything like that before that day. Imagine how that helped him when he was faced with a sudden job search eighteen months later.

Second, we are intentionally looking for ways to live together better. Understanding and knowing how to interact with different personalities can make a huge difference in a family dynamic. And while we did not have a whole lot of kid fighting before, I saw tremendous maturity in both kids as we moved into the teen years when communication is tough alongside its evil cousin, puberty. Enabling leadership at home has been a wonderful and refreshing thing for me as a business leader. I've taken pressure off myself to lead at all times because I've paved a path for my family to lead. Every member of my family leads our unit in some way, and that makes us stronger.

Finally, enabling leadership at home truly makes my home a respite—an island of rest. Let's face it, folks: our homes need leadership, just as our companies do. And just as we must be intentional to create the environment we want at work, I say that goes double for our homes. Don't just let anything go in your place of rest. Our homes should be our beacons for peace, not chaos. Stop right now and think of the last time you took intentional action to impact the dynamic of your home life.

- What did you do?
- What prompted that action?
- What was the result of your action? Was it positive or negative?
- Can you do anything to change it?

Regardless of your answer, think about things you do to improve life for your coworkers or direct reports at work. Could any of those efforts be replicated at home? Take some time from this point forward to be intentional about your home and family dynamic. No one owns that responsibility to set that course more than you. Spreading the responsibility of leadership across the family makes life easier for all and serves to develop the next generation of leaders today.

Chapter Three in Review: LEAD

1. Define Lead
   a. Origins/definition
   b. What's necessary to lead
2. Three Criteria to Leading Well
   a. Clarity
   b. Measurability
   c. Flexibility
3. Three Keys to Leading Well in a Matrixed Organization
   a. Identify, build, and grow key stakeholder relationships
   b. Manage downline more than upline
   c. Know who makes the ultimate decision
4. Enabling Leadership at Home

Chapter Three: LEAD Notes

CONCLUSION

Congratulations! You just finished a primer on how to make change happen wherever you lead. Whether it's at work, volunteering, or at home, change is bound to happen - that is a guarantee. At some point in life, you will want to drive change, or change will be thrust upon you, and you will need to lead through it.

Regardless of the project, industry, or timing, Engage, Collaborate, Lead is a relevant, proven method you can employ to drive any change you want within any organization. From Fortune 500 companies to local government agencies, Relationships Matter Now has worked at engaging team members by connecting their story to the greater story their organization is telling. We've collaborated with these entities to cocreate solutions to allow them to overcome challenges and reach strategic and fiduciary goals. And finally, we've ignited greater, more fulfilling leadership in all parties in the companies and organizations we've partnered with over the last four years.

Relationships Matter Now continues to grow today on the premise of Engage, Collaborate, Lead. We referenced that our fastest-growing segment of work has been inclusion and diversity strategy and programming over the last two years. We have quickly become leaders in this space, which has sorely needed innovation, because of the way we help companies and organizations take a fresh and collaborative look at diversity and inclusion. Since 1965, when the Equal Employment Opportunity Commission was formed as a directive of the Civil Rights Act of 1964, gargantuan efforts have worked to fulfill President John F. Kennedy's executive order requiring the government to take "affirmative action" to ensure that all Americans have an equal opportunity to apply for jobs and be employed and treated fairly during the course of their work. Both private and public sectors have extended millions upon millions of dollars and hours of energy to achieve a richly diverse workforce that reflects our country's rich diversity, yet we still have lots of work to do.

Compound the length of time and energy on the topic with the literal negative hijacking of the word *diversity* over the last decade, and you have a recipe for compliance-driven activities that never truly get at why diversity and inclusive behaviors in the workplace are imperative for our country's continued global leadership. The changing demographics of the United States as well as tons of empirical data that show that diversity drives bottom-line results have not been enough to sufficiently move the needle on this area for a host of reasons. And the clock is ticking on building a prepared workforce to replace our legion of one hundred million baby boomers leaving the workforce daily.

I humbly offer Engage, Collaborate, Lead as a possible solution.

Relationships Matter Now is already seeing great early results in companies and organizations in which we've implemented our methodology on inclusion and diversity strategy and programming. We lead companies through the murky waters of frank and bold discussion about diversity—what it means and why it matters. We partner to cocreate what inclusive behaviors in the workplace mean by organization - there is no silver bullet answer. We enable leadership at all levels to ensure the best possible outcomes of any inclusion and diversity activity and expenditure. We also get at the heart of the people who are impacted because, after all, behind every data point is a person - a story. And we tell more stories and connect them to bigger, greater stories so that we have a chance to cocreate solutions and innovate in ways that drive leadership. And it's working, folks.

Our client list in the inclusion and diversity space is growing daily, and we are working across organizations to spread our work method of Engage, Collaborate, Lead as the answer to driving success in diversifying workplaces that develop inclusive behaviors. Retail, media, higher education, energy, government, and nonprofit agencies have all experienced firsthand the transformative power of Engage, Collaborate, Lead in their diversity and inclusion efforts. Our founder is a highly rated presenter at the annual Forum on Workplace Inclusion, the country's oldest and largest conference dedicated to advancing diversity and inclusion practice hosted by the Opus College of Business at the University of St. Thomas in Minneapolis, MN. We are driving measurable change in organizations and leading the next discussion on inclusion and diversity in the United States, all because we subjected our own business to Engage, Collaborate, Lead in late 2013.

Once we pinpointed the language of our method, we brought Relationships Matter Now stakeholders to the table via videoconference to identify how to best grow the business going into 2014. Building on our success in organizational development and marketing projects, our team of contractors and our founder's personal board of directors used our own methodology to set a path and specific goals to build on the two diversity and inclusion projects we secured in 2013. The result of our four-hour self-reflection and brainstorming work session? A new stream of revenue and the very book you're reading.

***

Engage, Collaborate, Lead is really an exercise in self-reflection. We hope you've had a chance to connect your own story to the bigger story on our planet. Our desire is that you are now poised to go cocreate solutions to our planet's troubles. Most of all, we hope that you achieve your own higher purpose after going on this journey with us.

RESOURCES

Below are resources that inspired the creation of the Engage, Collaborate, Lead methodology.

Books
Change
   Switch: How to Change Things When Change Is Hard, by Chip and Dan Heath, 2010
Personal Change
   An Imperceptible Spark: Finding the Courage to Live a Life of Joy, by Steven Rice, 2011
Family Change
   The 3 Big Questions for a Frantic Family: A Leadership Fable about Restoring Sanity to the Most Important Organization in Your Life, by Patrick Lencioni, 2008
Challenging Things as They Are
   David and Goliath: Underdogs, Misfits and the Art of Battling Giants, by Malcolm Gladwell, 2014

Websites We Frequent
Harvard Business Review—www.hbr.org
Switch and Shift—www.switchandshift.com
Lead Change Group—www.leadchangegroup.com
The Mind Unleashed—www.themindunleashed.com
16 Personalities—www.16personalities.com/free-personality-test

Twitter Leaders We Follow
Bruce Kasanoff—@brucekasanoff
Baratunde Thurston—@baratunde
Stosh Walsh—@stoshdwalsh
Whitney Johnson—@johnsonwhitney
Frank Sonnenberg—@fsonnenberg
Rinku Sen—@rinkuwrites
Kathryn Finney—@kathrynfinney
Ed Batista—@edbatista
Joseph Grenny—@josephgrenny
Liz Wiseman—@lizwiseman
David Rendall—@daverendall
Shaun King—@shaunking
David McQueen—@davidmqueen

ACKNOWLEDGMENTS

To my social media acquaintance, business colleague, and later friend, Steven E. Rice: without you, *Engage, Collaborate, Lead* would not exist. Thank you for seeing me and my business in a way that I never could have imagined or dreamed. You are an amazing content specialist, and I look forward to many years of collaboration and success.

To each member of my personal board of directors—you have been with me over my lifetime, encouraging and bolstering me in many ways with your many talents. Many thousands of thanks for your love, support, and correction (in alphabetical order): Deanna Armentrout, Isael Barreto, Carlo Castilla, Steve Davidson, Kathy DeWitt, Phil Dillard, Jason Feldman, Chris Linder, Alicia Matheson, LeAnn Pauley Heard, Judy Pitchford, Shawntee Reed, Steven E. Rice, and Susan Reiter.

To my tribe, without whom there would be no inspiration to write or work: the calls, e-mails, likes, tweets, retweets, shares, prayers, hugs, and generally the great mojo and juju you send my way fuel me. I'd love to list all of you by name, but that would be another whole book, so I will only single out one—Lakesha Brown, my Twitter BFF who introduced me to Steven E. Rice. Thank you, my fellow entrepreneur and soul sister, for being in my life and contributing greatly to my work.

My growing client list that is over forty strong, resulting in close to seventy unique projects over the last four years: there are no favorites—I love each and every one of you the same. Thank you for being open to change and true transformation in your organizations.

My dad, Albert C. Wilmer Sr., who modeled for me an amazing work ethic that is the best thing (and worst thing, too - just being honest) about me, and for that, I thank you. My clients thank you as well.

My family, starting with my husband, Isael Barreto: I thank you for the last fourteen years of love, partnership, and sacrificial growth (individually and as a unit) and the wonderful family we've built together. We did this. We continue to do this. I love you and would not change a thing. To Emma, my firstborn—sensitive, bold, and confident leader child who is doing amazing things and will continue to do many more—and Evan, my strong communicator and the loving and intuitive boy who will quickly rule the world: I can't wait to watch you two grow. And if by chance I am not blessed to see it all the way to completion, *know* that I am with you always, just as my mom is with me.

My relationship with Jesus Christ, author and finisher of my faith, creator of the universe, and light of the world who loves me and keeps me going: thank you for allowing me the opportunity to serve you and everyone with the talents you gave me.

ABOUT THE AUTHOR

Denise W. Barreto is the managing partner and founder of Relationships Matter Now, LLC, a strategic business and marketing firm built on the "RMN Approach" of engagement, collaboration, and leadership.

You know your business best, and Denise knows how to bring your best to the forefront. Taking her experience as a corporate strategist with over twenty years of experience spanning a variety of industries, Denise has distilled her expertise working with some of the most recognized brands on the planet into a powerful system that you can leverage to bring out the best in your organization.

Denise's experience as a marketing expert with brands like AT&T, United Airlines, Pella, Sears Holdings, the Chicago Fire Major League Soccer Team, and the US Soccer Federation uniquely positions her to guide your organization through growth in a way that engages your team, identifies the values and priorities of the organization, and allows the best you have to offer to shine through.

Personal leadership is just as vital as organizational leadership, and Denise has excelled professionally and personally. She was elected to the board of trustees for the Village of Lake in the Hills, Illinois, in 2009 and again in 2013. In 2014, she was appointed by Governor Pat Quinn to the Illinois Business Enterprise Program Council. The council helps implement, monitor, and enforce the goals of the business enterprise program for minorities, females, and persons with disabilities.

Since 2001, Denise has been married to Isael Barreto and is therefore "Mexican by marriage." She is mom to Emma, thirteen, and Evan, nine, and is the proud owner of a feisty dachshund named Chica. When she is not leading in her business or other personal endeavors, she and her family can be found enjoying life on many adventures while traveling in the United States, Mexico, and other destinations in the Caribbean and Europe or eating a hot pot in Chicago's Chinatown.

www.ingramcontent.com/pod-product-compliance
Lightning Source LLC
Chambersburg PA
CBHW071754170526
45167CB00003B/1027